Who Controls The Earth; God Or The Devil?

(God, Man & The Devil)

KOJO KRONZUWA YANKSON

Who Controls The World - God or The Devil?
Copyright 2015
Kojo Kronzuwa Yankson

Book Cover designed by: Samuel Budu-Manuel

Published by
Centre for Leadership Influence
6700 Belcrest Rd. Apt 1122. Hyattsville, 20782 MD

For information or to order books, please email:
s_yankson@hotmail.com.
Tel: +1301-276-1956

ISBN:978-9988-2-2811-8
Printed in Ghana
All Rights Reserve

CONTENTS

Acknowledgements

This book is the collective effort of many. Among them are Dr Deborah Alema-Mensah who is my constant support and Dr (Mrs) Ekua Anowah Amponsah Agyemang. I am grateful for their encouragement, vital criticisms and contributions.

Finally, my appreciation to my mum: Elizabeth, siblings: Ato, Vida, Tony, Nana Kwaaba, Andrew, and friends: Rhoda Hanson, Pastor Crabbe and Maame Afua Acquah for their confidence in my abilities.

Introduction

This book is part of a series titled: God, Man and the Devil. The intention of writing this series is to give a systematic insight into the relationship that exist between God, Man, and devil. This is to make it possible for christians to give a practical explanation to the questions that bother them.

This book seeks to answer the question, "Who controls the world - God or the Devil?" This question is being asked because of the strife between good and evil. This book will juxtapose the authority and control of God on earth and the authority and control of the devil on earth. A snapshot of the chapters that make up the book are explained below.

Chapter one explains how the free will nature of man led to the first battle between God and the devil. (The eternal struggle between good and evil.)

Chapter two discusses God's plans to redeem the control of the earth from the devil and why God had to delay the implementation of his plans until the reign of the Roman Empire.

Chapter three discusses the challenges Jesus Christ faced when he came to the earth and why he had to die the way he died in order to save man.

Chapter four explains why the blood of Jesus Christ is the only thing that redeems man from sin and death. Couldn't God have used anything apart from the blood of Jesus?

Chapter five explains why the death of Jesus Christ on the cross had to be facilitated by a traitor (Judas Iscariot) and false accusers.

Chapter six explains why at the mention of the name of Jesus, every knee should bow, be it on earth or in heaven. This chapter also explains what christians must do to maintain the authority of Jesus on earth.

Chapter seven explains why Jesus has total authority on earth but not total control. It also explains the steps being taken by Jesus Christ to obtain total control over the earth.

Chapter eight explains the importance of the last battle prophesied to take place between Jesus and the devil. It will be a battle for control over man and the earth.

Chapter nine discusses what every christian should do to secure an inheritance with God after they die.

This introduction is a teaser to the concept underlying the book. It is recommended that readers would read the book in detail to get a full understanding of the one who controls the earth.

Chapter One

The First Battle For Man And The Earth

Man was created by God to have a free will - that is the power of choice.[1] He was neither created a subject for God nor a subject for the devil. The free will nature of man when he was created gave rise to the potential for either God or the devil to establish a domineering influence over man. The reason being that a decision by man to be righteous would give God a domineering influence over man while a decision by man to be unrighteous would give the devil a domineering influence over man.

The battle for man was also the battle for the earth. This is because God, after creation gave the authority of the earth to man. As such, anyone who controlled man, automatically controlled the earth. The earth is a sovereign territory separate from heaven. God, after creation, kept control of the heavens and gave man authority over the earth through Adam.[2] God is not a bully.[3] He abides by the laws and

---

[1] Deuteronomy 30:19
[2] Genesis 1:26

2

the commandments that he sets. That is why it is said that, "... thou hast magnified thy word above all thy name."[4]

God will not interfere with the management of the earth without the permission of man. It is for this reason that God has to win the loyalty of man in order to control the earth. It became necessary for God to pursue an agenda to win the loyalty of man because of the devil's quest to do so. The devil's motive for wanting to win the loyalty of man was to challenge the authority of God through man. God, on the other hand, needed to win the loyalty of man so he could have fellowship with man and be a father to man.

God began his quest to win the loyalty of man and control the earth by admonishing man not to the fruits from the tree of knowledge of good and evil.[5] The devil on the other hand,

[3] Revelations 3:20
[4] Palm 138:2
[5] Genesis 2:9,16&17

began his quest by persuading man to eat of the tree of knowledge of good and evil.[6] Man had an option to yield to the devil or eat from the tree of life. The tree of life (nature of life). was to grant man the intelligence to know the difference between what is right and what is wrong and empower man with the tendency to choose right over wrong.

The opposite can be said of the tree of knowledge of good and evil (nature of death). The nature of death was to empower man with the tendency to choose wrong over right. Man gave in to the enticement of the devil and ate from the tree of knowledge of good and evil. The disobedience of Adam resulted in the inability of God to extend his kingdom on earth.

Adam's actions disappointed God. He responded to their disobedience by ejecting them from the Garden of Eden and pronouncing this judgment on them: "I will

---

[6] Genesis 3:3-5

greatly multiply thy sorrow and thy conception; in sorrow thou shalt bring forth children; and thy desire shall be to thy husband, and he shall rule over thee."[7]

One may ask: Why didn't God allow man to stay in the Garden of Eden and eat from the tree of life after man had eaten from the tree of knowledge of good and evil and died? I ask this question because, if man had eaten from the tree of life it would have given man a nature of life alongside the nature of death. God did not allow this because it would have created an abomination out of man. An abomination because two opposite elements cannot dwell in the same place (it can only occur in transition).[8] One cannot be both dead and alive neither can one be both cold and hot.

---

[7] Genesis 3:16
[8] John 1:5, Romans 13:12, 1 Corinthians 15:50, 2Corianthians 6:14.

Chapter Two

The Sinful Nature Of Man

"... death reigned from Adam to Moses, even over them that had not sinned after the similitude of Adam's transgression... [9]" Man died, the moment he ate from the tree of knowledge of good and evil. This kind of death meant that - man had become vulnerable to choose evil over good. This gave the devil control over Adam and all his descendants. The devil's authority stretched over every man irrespective of where that man's loyalty lay.

Man became corrupted with adultery, fornication, idolatry, witchcraft, hatred, wrath, strife, envy, murder and drunkenness when death took control of man.[10] The vices listed above and many others like them are the reasons for all of man's problems. We are all victims in one way or the other of the effect of the vices of death. If it is not theft, it is divorce, if it is not murder, it is blackmail, if it is not a cheating husband, it is a cheating wife,

---

[9] Romans 5:14
[10] Galatians 5:19-21

if it is not rape, it is bribery.

These vices created a situation that made it difficult for God to relate to man in person. He had to relate to Man mainly through angels. This situation made it necessary for God to reconcile with man and take back the control of the earth. God, on this basis, decided to send his only begotten son Jesus Christ to the earth to save man. Jesus was to save man by establishing the Kingdom of God on earth. God took this decision because of his love for man. Despite this decision, Jesus could not come during the era of Adam and Eve.[11] Because, the people in that era were not mentally and institutionally prepared for his assignment. His assignment required that - kingly and priesthood institutions be established on the earth before it could be fulfilled. The priesthood institution was to help man understand Jesus' redemptive assignment - shed his blood to save man.

---

[11] Revelations 13:8

While the kingly institution was to help man understand the role of Jesus as their king.

God began his quest to prepare man for Jesus' assignment by introducing Abel, the second son of Adam to the principle of first fruit. First fruit is a ritual which forms part of the priesthood institution. This initiative by God was short-lived when Cain killed Abel. He killed him out of jealousy when his sacrifice was rejected and that of Abel was accepted by God. Evil spread throughout the earth after the death of Abel until the whole earth became corrupt. Evil was firmly in control of the world at this point, and the plan of God to redeem man was in danger.

Noah, his three sons and their wives were the only exception to the corruption at the time. God therefore had to act to protect them and the future of humanity. He responded to the evil in the world by destroying all that lived on the surface of the earth through a flood, saving only Noah, his family and some animals by an ark.

God made progress with this plan to build a kingly and priesthood institution after the flood; when Nimrod established the first empire in the history of the Bible. The Bible refers to Nimrod as a mighty hunter before the Lord.[12] He was a great grandson of Noah. This progress was stalled when Nimrod rebelled against God by building the tower of Babel to challenge the authority of God.

God responded to his rebellion by confusing the language of the citizens of his empire. Each member of the empire began to speak a different language. This curtailed the rebellion and destroyed the empire of Nimrod. But the kingly institution was preserved. Generations after Nimrod have made use of the kingly institution till date. God, at this moment, was

---

[12] Genesis 10:9, Genesis 6:13-18

through with the first part of his plan. What was left was for a priesthood institution to be established among men.

The world before Moses experienced isolated practices of the rituals that constitute the priesthood institution. Some of these isolated practices occurred under Abel, Noah, Abraham and Jethro (Moses' father-in-law.) Abel performed a priesthood ritual when he brought the firstlings (first fruit) of his produce unto the Lord. Noah performed a priesthood ritual when he offered a burnt offering unto the Lord in appreciation of God for saving them from the flood. Abraham on the other hand, performed a priesthood ritual when he paid tithe to Melchisedech, king of Salem, priest of the Most High God.

All these isolated executions of priesthood rituals were in preparation towards the establishment of the priesthood institution through which Jesus would fulfil his assignment. God, through Moses, established the priesthood institution among the Israelites and made Aaron the first high priest. This completed God's quest to prepare man and the earth for Jesus to come and fulfil his assignment. Nevertheless, Jesus Christ would not come to the earth until after about 800 years. This allowed these institutions to be firmly established both in practise and in the minds of the people.

Chapter Three

The Second Battle For Man
And The Earth

Jesus Christ was given birth to by a virgin. His life on earth was met by many attempts to sabotage his assignment without success. One of such attempts was when Herod killed all the first born - male children - who were born in Israel around the time that Jesus was born. He did this with the intention of killing the infant Jesus in the process but he failed.[13] He failed because God, through an angel, gave Joseph foreknowledge about his plan.

Jesus Christ began his assignment by preaching about the kingdom of God, healing the sick, and casting out demons. The climax of his assignment was his death on the cross. For Jesus' death to achieve its purpose, he had to die in place of Barabbas, a man convicted of a crime punishable by death. Trading places with such a man was necessary so he could pay the price for man's freedom and destroy the works of the devil in the process.[14]

Jesus Christ died in place of a sinful man when the Jews opted to crucify him instead of Barabbas.

---

[13] 1John 3:8
[14] 1Peter 2:22-24

Barabbas was a man convicted of murder. He, dying in place of Barabbas, took on the sins of Barabbas and all men.

This gave Barabbas and man the opportunity to gain their freedom from sin. Without trading places with Barabbas, Jesus Christ would not have died a sinful death and he would not have been able to liberate man.

The death of Jesus Christ bears the same significance as the sheep and goat that were sacrificed in the era of Moses and Aaron to redeem the Israelites from sin and death. The men whose sin had to be forgiven in the era of Moses and Aaron, traded places with the sacrificed sheep or goat so they could be cleansed.

Jesus invaded hell and conquered death when he died. Death and hell took on a prisoner they could not hold. The keeper of the prison of death surrendered the keys of the prison to him. "I am he that liveth, and was dead; and, behold, I am alive for evermore, Amen; and have the keys of hell and of death" are the words of Jesus after conquering death.[15]

"But we speak the wisdom of God in a mystery, even the hidden wisdom, which God ordained before the world unto our glory: Which none of the princes of this world knew: for had they known it, they would not have crucified the Lord of glory."[16] It can be deduced that, if the devil knew that he would not have been able to hold Jesus Christ prisoner, he would not have crucified Him. In conclusion, his death and resurrection resulted in the deliverance of man from sin and death, and the defeat of the devil.

---

[15] Revelation 1:18
[16] 1Corinthians 2:7-8

Chapter Four

Why Blood?

Jesus died to shed his blood to redeem man from sin and death. Why should the blood of Jesus be the thing to redeem man from sin and death? [17] Couldn't God have used anything aside the blood of Jesus? This question can be answered based on the law of Unity of Opposites. According to the law of Unity of Opposites, every element in the universe is created in pairs and each pair is made up of two opposites. Examples are: man and woman, dry and wet, hot and cold, life and death.

No element can possess the characteristic of the two opposites that make up a pair.[18] Each element in a pair exists at the expense of the other. You cannot be cold and hot simultaneously. Neither can one be alive and dead at the same time. It is abnormal for one to be both dead and alive simultaneously. To be dead, one must give up life. In the same way, to be hot, one must give up coldness. Based on this analysis, one can conclude that there is a trade-off relationship between the two opposite elements that make up every pair.

---

[17] 1 Corinthians 15:50, 2 Corinthians 6:14
[18] 1 Corinthians 15:50, 2 Corinthians 6:14

It is on the basis of this trade-off that God instituted the sacrifice of life to redeem man from death. This is because life is the opposite of death. For man to come back to life from death after the sin of Adam, man had to trade places with something that had life. It is for this reason that animals without blemish were slaughtered under the law of Moses to redeem man from sin and death. It is for the same reason that Jesus had to die to give man life. Jesus was chosen because he was without sin. The life of an animal or man is in his blood. That is why the Bible says, "And almost all things are by the law purged with blood; and without shedding of blood there is no remission."[19]

The use of animals in sacrifices to attain righteousness under the Law of Moses is said to be by works. It is by works because the sinner provided the sacrifice (lamb or fowls). and had to perform some rituals before his sins could be purged. For example, the sinner had to lay his hands on the head of his sacrifice or the animal to be sacrificed in the presence of the Lord and the priest, and confess his sins before his sins could be

---

[19]Hebrews 9:22, Leviticus 17:11

purged.[20] The people who could not afford to buy the animals for their sins to be purged were deprived of salvation under this system. It is because of this reason that Jesus came to die to abolish the system of using animals to atone for sins.

Righteousness by Jesus is a gift. It's a gift because the sacrifice for the atonement of the sins of the sinner is provided on behalf of the sinner.

Jesus Christ is the sacrifice for his atonement. The sinner plays no part in his atonement - he only needs to accept the work done for him by Jesus on the cross. That is why it is said that: "For it is by God's grace that you have been saved through faith. It is not the result of your own efforts, but God's gift, so that no one can boast about it."[21]

---

[20] Leviticus 4:27-35
[21]Ephesians 2:8-9(Good News Bible)

Chapter Five

The Traitor And The False Accusers

The assignment of Jesus Christ was designed to avoid violence and legal errors - God did not want to stand accused of any wrong doing. Every event that contributed to his death and resurrection was designed to avoid violence and legal errors. Two of such events were the roles of the traitor and that of the false accusers.

The Traitor

The High priest and his crew were reluctant to arrest and crucify Jesus Christ because they feared the reaction of his followers: "And the scribes and chief priests heard it, and sought how they might destroy him: for they feared him, because all the people were astonished at his doctrine."[22] The High Priest and his crew therefore engaged Judas Iscariot to lead them to arrest Jesus Christ in the absence of his followers, "And he promised, and sought opportunity to betray him unto them in the absence of the multitude."[23]

Did Judas Iscariot sin by betraying Jesus Christ? This question is being asked because Judas Iscariot's betrayal aided Jesus to fulfil his

---

[22]Mark-11:18
[23] Luke 22:6

assignment. He sinned because, "All unrighteousness is sin..."[24]

If it was a sin, then why did God choose Judas Iscariot to play the role of betraying Jesus? God chose him because he was a thief and a traitor.[25] God only used his expertise as a traitor and a thief to help Jesus to fulfil his assignment. Jesus was only one of Judas' many victims.

Did Judas have an option to refuse the role of betraying Jesus Christ? The option was for him to abandon the life of a thief and a traitor. Another person with Judas' expertise would have been found to play the role of betraying Jesus.

Without Judas, it would have been difficult, if not impossible, for the High Priest and his crew to arrest

and crucify Jesus Christ. This is because the followers of Jesus Christ would not have allowed

---

[24] 1 John 5:17, Matthew 26:24-25
[25] John 12:4-6

him to be arrested. It would have resulted in violence if force was applied. And this would have made it difficult for Jesus Christ to fulfil his assignment. This conclusion is not in any way suggesting that God had no options as to how to get Jesus crucified, aside betrayal.

The False Accusers

"For he hath made him to be sin for us, who knew no sin; that we might be made the righteousness of God in him."[26] It can be deduced from the scripture above that, Jesus Christ needed to die a sinner's death to be able to liberate man. The question is, on what grounds was he going to be convicted and killed as a sinner since he was a man without sin? The Jews had two options from which to convict and kill him. These two options were: for them to either convict and kill him by false accusation or convict and kill him by factual evidence.

Conviction by false accusation was the only option left for Jesus Christ to die a sinner's death. This

---

[26] 2Corontines 5:21

happened with the help of the false witnesses. The High Priest and some elders got people to accuse Jesus Christ falsely and got him crucified.[27] They accused him of perverting the nation and refusing to pay tax.[28] Without the false accusers, it would have been illegal for Jesus Christ to be arrested and crucified.

Conviction by factual evidence would have been impossible since Jesus Christ never broke the law or sinned.[29] His innocence was confirmed when Pontius Pilate sought to release him against the will of the High Priest and his crew.[30]

---

[27] Matthew 26:60-65

Chapter Six

Jesus Christ The King

God has always had his agents on earth, the same can be said of the devil. God uses prophets, priests, and kings as agents to execute his programmes on earth. The devil on the other hand, uses idol worshipers and evil - minded people to execute his agenda. The devil, until his defeat by Jesus Christ on the cross, was the prince of the earth.[28]

The authority over the earth passed to Jesus when he defeated the devil on the cross. This made Jesus the automatic King over the earth. It is therefore a legal obligation for all the inhabitants of the earth (Man, the devil and all other things) to submit to the authority of Jesus. That is why "...at the name of Jesus every knee should bow, of things in heaven, and things in earth, and things under the earth."[29] The inhabitants of the earth have no option but to obey the name of Jesus; because there is nowhere in the universe where the authority of Jesus does not extend.

Every kingdom requires a land, people and a king

---

[28] John 12:31
[29] Philippians 2:10

to be established. The king owns the land and all that is in it. The subjects who live in the kingdom must obey the king by reason of living on the land of the king. Anybody who lives on the territory of the kingdom and dislikes the king must relocate to another kingdom or risk being charged with treason if found not to be on the same page with the king. In an absolute monarchy, the word of the king is law - He has absolute authority and should be opposed with utmost caution.

The authority of the king is often exercised through his name. This is done, either by word of mouth or by a written document. Anybody who receives a document or a message in the name of the king is obliged to obey. It is treason to oppose the authority of the King. Let us therefore walk in this confidence as christians that the devil and his agents are obliged to submit to the authority and name of Jesus Christ.

One must note that the devil and his agents will not submit to the Lordship of Jesus willingly. They have to be forced to do so[30]. It is the responsibility of christians to act as the law enforcing agents of the kingdom of God and ensure that the name of Jesus Christ is obeyed in every part of the earth. Christians must do this with power through prayer and knowledge. Prayer is a tool required to empower the christian with energy so he could enforce the laws of the kingdom of God. The more one prays the more energy one is empowered with to fight oppositions to the kingdom of God.

The spirit of man needs constant energy from prayer and the word of God to survive - in the same way that the body needs constant energy from food to survive. This is because it is the energy generated from prayer and the word of God that the spirit of man uses for its operations. Some of the operations of the spirit are fighting sickness, and enforcing other rights of the christian. Some of such rights are: divine provision, joy, and divine health. The constant use of energy by the spirit of man makes it difficult for the spirit to hold on to any energy gained through prayer. That is whythe Bible admonishes christians to pray without ceasing.[31]

---

[30] Ephesians6:11
[31] 1 Thessalonians 5:17

"My people are destroyed for lack of knowledge..."[32] The knowledge supplied to the mind - engineers it, and transforms it from one level of value to the other. It is the bridge between the wise and the foolish, the strong and the weak, the rich and the poor, the righteous and the unrighteous, the superior and the inferior. If christians are to control the world - they must be voracious learners. This is because no individual is better than the other except for the knowledge he is exposed to.

One should be mindful about the knowledge one encounters. This is because knowledge could either degrade or enhance. Knowledge from superior minds will guarantee you superior results. The Bible contains the most superior knowledge in the world. It is God's mind in print. Better understanding of the Bible by christians will guarantee them power over the evil and the world. Other books must be read to compliment the knowledge one gets from the Bible. Per this understanding, christians must continually pray

---

[32] Hosea 4:6

and acquire knowledge in order to maintain and advance their control on earth through the name of Jesus Christ.[33]

.

---

[33] The last two paragraphs are extracts from: Kojo Kronzuwa Yankson(2015). How To Achieve A High Performing Mind, Ghana

Chapter Seven

The Third Battle For Man And The Earth

Jesus Christ is the second man after Adam to gain total authority over the earth. This he achieved when he defeated the devil. He has authority over the entire earth but not total control. This is because not everybody is willing to accept Him as their Lord and King.

Jesus owns the earth and all that are in it because the earth and all that are in it was created through him and for him[34]. He therefore has the right to defend his property. Jesus has given all men until the time of the great tribulation and the war of Armageddon to repent and accept him as their Lord and saviour - and become law - abiding citizens of the kingdom of God or face judgment and expulsion from the surface of the earth.[35] It is necessary for Jesus to wage war on those who will not accept him because two captains cannot navigate one ship. The earth cannot continue to be ruled by good (God) and evil (Satan.)

The strategy adopted by Jesus Christ to fight and defeat the devil and his agents is the great tribulation and the war of Armageddon. The great

---

[34] I Colossians 1:16
[35] Revelation 19:19-21

tribulation is series of activities designed to torment the people who will be living on earth after the rapture.[36] The rapture is an evacuation plan designed by God to evacuate the followers of Jesus Christ from the earth before the great tribulation and the war of Armageddon. The people who will be living on the earth after the rapture are the people who have refused to accept Jesus as their Lord and personal saviour.

Jesus Christ will descend on earth with a host of angels and defeat the anti-Christ and his false prophets who have decided not to submit to his lordship in the war of Armageddon.[37] This war will take place after the great tribulation, The defeated anti-Christ and his false prophets will be locked up in hell forever.[38] Until this battle is fought, the control of the earth will continue to be a tussle between God and the devil.

---

[36] Revelation 16:1-21
[37] Revelation 19:11-21
[38] Revelation 20:10

Chapter Eight

The Fourth And Final Battle For The Earth

The devil and his agent after the war of Armageddon will be arrested and put in chains for a period of thousand years[39] - while the people that will remain on earth after the war of Armageddon will be ruled by Jesus Christ for a period of thousand years. Jesus Christ will rule the world with the saints who were raptured to heaven.[40]

The people that will remain on the earth after the war of Armageddon will be obliged to obey the laws of God. Jesus Christ will rule the world from Jerusalem.[41] Anybody who will disobey the rule of Jesus Christ will be punished. His rule will be characterised by peace.[42]

The devil will be released from prison by God after thousand years. The reason for the release of the devil is for him to test the loyalty of the people who remain on earth after the war of Armageddon to Jesus Christ. The test is to prove whether they have repented from their evil ways or their obedience to Jesus during the thousand years was a sham.

---

[39] Revelation 20:1-3
[40] Revelation 20: 6
[41] Isaiah 2:1- 4
[42] Isaiah 11:1-9

The people will be deceived by Satan. The deceived people will join forces with the devil and rebel against the rule of Jesus. Jesus will in return fight and defeat them.

The defeated devil and his followers will be put in hell forever.[43] God will create a new earth and a new heaven after this final battle for Jesus Christ and his followers to live on forever.[44] God will also give man a new body that will enable man to overcome the corrupt nature and habits that bedevilled him after the fall of Adam.

.

---

[43] Revelation 20: 7-10
[44] Revelation 21:1-5

Chapter Nine

Reward

Jesus Christ before his death and resurrection, had authority in heaven as the son of God but had no authority on the earth. The earth was given to man by God to dominate. For Jesus to wield authority over the earth, he had to take the form of a man. Any personality aside man who wants to wield authority on earth has to do that through a man or be born unto the earth as a man.

"And being found in fashion as a man, he humbled himself, and became obedient unto death, even the death of the cross. Wherefore God also hath highly exalted him, and given him a name which is above every name: That at the name of Jesus every knee should bow, of things in heaven, and things in earth, and things under the earth"[45]

It can be deduced from the scripture above that Jesus Christ had no sovereign authority in heaven or on earth before fulfiling his assignment on the cross. The fulfillment of His assignment was critical for him to receive his inheritance as a sovereign authority in the heavens and on the

---

[45] Philippians 2:8-10

earth.

His position as a sovereign authority in the heavens and on the earth did not come to him by chance. He had to defeat the devil and reconcile man to God to merit that position.

Before completing this assignment, the only accolade Jesus Christ had was that, he is the only begotten son of God. The phrase, "the only begotten son of God"[46] means that Jesus Christ is the only son of God created by God himself. Adam is also a son of God from birth but was created through Jesus Christ.[47]

God is no respecter of persons.[48] Christians should note that if Jesus Christ did not receive any inheritance from God until he completed his assignment, even so, no christian will receive any inheritance from God except he fulfils his responsibilities as a christian. "And, behold, I come quickly; and my reward is with me, to give every man according as his work shall be."[49]

---

[46] John 1:18
[47] Colossians 1:16, Luke 6:38
[48] Acts 10:34
[49] Revelations-22:12

The great commission is the work required by God for every christian to undertake in order to be rewarded by God. The responsibility of the christian under the great commission is for the christian to continue the redemptive work of Jesus Christ. This can be achieved by making disciples of the world for God through the preaching of the kingdom of God.[50]

This we must do as christians until the final battle against the devil is won. Christians who preach the kingdom of God - share the sufferings of God - as a result, will share in his inheritance.[51]

---

[50] Matthew 28:19-20
[51] 1 Peter 4:13

Other Books By The Author

- How To Achieve A High Performing Mind

- The Journey From Wakanda To Wakanda

ABOUT THE AUTHOR

The author of this book is a preacher, a thinker, a business consultant, and a researcher at the Centre for Leadership Influence.

Kojo Kronzuwa Yankson
Financial Economist (ACE)
Qualified Accountant (ACCA)
Project Management Professional (PMP)
Certified In Risk And Information Systems Control (CRISC)

www.ingramcontent.com/pod-product-compliance
Lightning Source LLC
Chambersburg PA
CBHW071936020426
42331CB00010B/2893